Cauliflower Rice Recipes

Replacing Traditional Rice with Low Carb Cauliflower Rice

Copyright

Copyright 2019 New Wave Publishing. All rights reserved under International and Pan-American Copyright Conventions. No rights granted to reproduce this book or portions thereof in any form or manner whatsoever without the express written permission of the copyright owner(s).

Legal Notice

Content in this book is provided "As Is". The authors and publishers provide no guarantees regarding results of any advice or recommendations contained herein. Much of this book is based on personal experiences of the author(s) and anecdotal evidence. Although the author and publisher have made reasonable attempts to for accuracy in the content, they assume no responsibility for its veracity, or for any errors or omissions. Nothing in this book is intended to replace common sense, medical, legal or other professional advice. This book is meant only to be informative and entertaining. Encore Books and its authors shall not be liable in the event of incidental or consequential damages in connection with, or arising out of, the providing of the information offered herein.

Any trademarks, service marks, product names or named features are assumed to be the property of their respective owners, and are used herein for reference purposes only. This book was not prepared, approved, licensed, or endorsed by any of the owners of the trademarks or brand names referred to in this book. There is no implied endorsement for any products or services mentioned in this publication.

Get Free Recipe eBooks!
Cookbook Club

Fabulous Free eBook Cookbooks Every Week!

Our eBooks are FREE for the first few days publication. Be the first to know when new books are published. Our collection includes hundreds of books on topics including healthy foods, diets, food allergy alternatives, gourmet meals, desserts, and easy and inexpensive meals.

Join the mailing list at:
EncoreBookClub.com

Related Books
Appetizers
http://url80.com/appetizers
Boozy Desserts
http://url80.com/boozy
Crazy for Cupcakes
http://url80.com/cupcakes
Fair Foods
http://url80.com/fair
Guacamole
http://url80.com/guacamole
Scones
http://url80.com/scones
Smoothies
http://url80.com/smoothies
Sriracha
http://url80.com/sriracha
Ramen Recipes
http://url80.com/ramen
Porkalicious
http://url80.com/porkalicious
Pudding
http://url80.com/pudding
The Awesome Avocado
http://url80.com/avocado

Table of Contents

CREATING RICE 1

BREAKFAST 2

- SAUSAGE AND CAULIFLOWER BREAKFAST BAKE 3
- CORNED BEEF AND CAULIFLOWER HASH 5
- CAULIFLOWER AND FETA OMELETTE 6
- CAULIFLOWER BREAD WITH CRISPY BACON, POACHED EGGS & AVOCADO ... 7
- CAULIFLOWER AND SPINACH BREAKFAST BREAD 9
- CAULIFLOWER BREAKFAST MUFFINS 10
- CAULIFLOWER PANCAKES 11
- CARAMEL CAULIFLOWER RICE FRITTATA 12

APPETIZERS & SIDES 13

- CAULIFLOWER PIZZA CRUST 14
- CAULIFLOWER SOUP 15
- CARROT AND CORIANDER SOUP WITH CAULIFLOWER RICE CRUMB ... 17
- CURRIED CAULIFLOWER RICE KALE SOUP 19
- CAULIFLOWER CHOWDER 21
- CAULIFLOWER TABBOULEH SALAD 22
- ITALIAN ROASTED CAULIFLOWER SALAD 23
- ROASTED CAULIFLOWER WITH AVOCADO LIME CILANTRO DRESSING ... 24
- INDIAN CAULIFLOWER FRIED RICE WITH ROASTED CHICKPEAS 25
- HONEY LIME SRIRACHA GLAZED CAULIFLOWER WINGS 27
- BUFFALO CAULIFLOWER BITES 28
- CAULIFLOWER RICE MAKI ROLLS 29
- CAULIFLOWER MUSHROOM RISOTTO 31
- CAULIFLOWER FRIED RICE 32
- CAJUN CAULIFLOWER RICE 33
- CAULIFLOWER RICE TURKEY STUFFING 35
- ASIAN CAULIFLOWER RICE LETTUCE CUPS 37
- CREAMY MASHED CAULIFLOWER 38
- CRISPY ORANGE CAULIFLOWER 39
- PAELLA WITH CAULIFLOWER RICE 41
- ROASTED SWEET POTATO AND CAULIFLOWER RICE COLLARD WRAPS ... 43
- GREEN CHILE CAULIFLOWER CASSEROLE 44

Mexican Cauliflower Rice	45
Cabbage Roll Skillet Casserole	46
Low Carb Keto Cheesy Cheddar Cauliflower Rice	47
Cauliflower Bacon Fritters	48
Baked Cauliflower Tater Tots	49
Cauliflower Mac and Cheese	51

ENTREES 52

Cauliflower Rice Tortillas	53
Spanish Chicken with Cauliflower Rice	54
Shrimp & Cauliflower Grits	55
Cauliflower Chickpea Masala Burgers	57
Cheesy Cauliflower Rice with Broccoli and Chicken	59
Coconut Curry Chicken Meatballs with Cauliflower Rice	61
Chicken Enchilada Rice Bowls	63
Mediterranean Cauliflower Rice	65
Thai Chicken Cauliflower Rice	66
Beef Burrito Bowls with Cilantro Lime Rice	67
Jambalaya	69
Gumbo and Rice	71

DESSERTS 73

Cauliflower Rice Pudding	74
Cauliflower Chocolate Pudding	75
Chocolate Cauliflower Bars	76
Chewy Chocolate Chip Cookies with Cauliflower	77

Creating Rice

Cauliflower is a very healthy and highly versatile vegetable. You can buy this cruciferous vegetable in "rice" form or turn a whole head into "rice" at home.

Because traditional rice often leaves dishes heavy, it's also wonderful to substitute a vegetable where this starch would usually be in a recipe. Its's a super way to squeeze more servings of vegetables into your day.

For do-it-yourselfers, there are two methods for turning your head of cauliflower into cauliflower rice. One method is using a box grater with medium-sized holes, the type of grater you often use to grate cheese. The second method uses a food processor fitted with a shape blade. Cut the cauliflower into florets or large chunks and place in processor. Pulse in 12 to 15 one-second pulses until it looks like rice.

Breakfast

Sausage and Cauliflower Breakfast Bake

Prep Time: 30 minutes
Cooking Time: 30 minutes
Servings: 8

Ingredients

- 1 teaspoon Italian seasoning
- ½ pound Italian-seasoned chicken or turkey sausage, casings removed
- 1 head cauliflower, medium-sized; cut into quarters; slicing the stem and leaves away and cut away the core from each quarter with an angled cut. Cut into small; bite-sized florets
- 2 cups chicken broth
- 1 cup Mozzarella cheese, shredded
- 1 pound boneless chicken breasts, cut into bite-size pieces
- 4 garlic cloves, minced
- 1 can Italian-seasoned tomatoes, crushed (28-ounce)
- ½ cup Parmesan cheese, grated
- 1 tablespoon olive oil
- Freshly ground pepper & sea salt to taste
- 1 medium onion, diced (approximately 1 cup)

Directions

1. Lightly grease a large-sized baking dish, 9x13" with some olive oil and preheat your oven to 350 F in advance.
2. Place half of the florets in a food processor container attached with a metal blade. Cover & pulse a couple of times until you get riced-cauliflower like consistency. Repeat this step with the leftover half.
3. Over high heat in a large pot; heat the chicken broth until starts boiling. Add in the riced-cauliflower; cover & let boil for a minute or two. Decrease the heat to medium; cook until cauliflower is soft, but not chewy, for 10 to 15 minutes. Immediately remove from the heat source & drain into a fine-meshed strainer pressing on the cauliflower gently to remove any excess liquid; set aside.
4. Over medium-high heat in a large skillet; heat the olive oil until hot. Add in the sausage and chicken. Cook until the meats are cooked through, for 8 to 12 minutes, breaking up the sausage using a large spoon. Add in the garlic, onion & Italian seasoning. Sauté for a couple of minutes, stirring every now and then; as you sauté the ingredients, don't forget to scrape up the brown bits. Stir in the crushed tomatoes & cook until sauce has decreased by one-third, for 10 to 15 minutes. Turn off the heat; taste and adjust the amount of seasonings to your preference.
5. Add the cauliflower to the skillet; give everything a good stir until evenly combined. Spread the mixture in the baking dish & evenly distribute. Evenly sprinkle with Parmesan and Mozzarella cheeses on top. Place in the middle of your oven & bake until the sauce starts bubbling and heated through, for 20 to 25 minutes. Let stand for 5 minutes before serving.

Corned Beef and Cauliflower Hash

Prep Time: 15 minutes
Cooking Time: 25 minutes
Servings: 4

Ingredients

- 16 ounces cauliflower rice (approximately 4 cups)
- 8 large eggs
- 1 small onion, diced
- 8 ounces turkey sausage
- 3 tablespoons water
- ⅛ teaspoon ground pepper
- 2 garlic cloves, minced
- 4 teaspoons olive oil, divided
- ¼ teaspoon salt

Directions

1. Over medium heat in a large nonstick skillet; heat 2 teaspoons of oil until hot. Add garlic and onion; cook until translucent, stirring frequently.
2. Add in the sausage & cook for 3 to 5 minutes, until cooked through, stirring frequently. Transfer the mixture to a large plate.
3. Raise the heat to medium-high & add in the cauliflower rice in an even layer. Cook for a couple of minutes, until it begins to turn golden brown, without stirring.
4. Stir & add pepper, water and salt. Cover & cook for 3 to 4 minutes, until tender & golden. Stir the sausage mixture back in & cook for 2 minutes, until heated through.
5. Now, over medium heat in a medium-sized nonstick skillet; heat a teaspoon of oil until hot; swirl to coat the bottom completely.
6. Break 4 eggs into the hot pan & cook for 2 to 3 minutes, until the whites are set but the yolks are still runny. Transfer to a plate & repeat with the leftover oil and eggs.
7. Evenly divide the hash among 4 plates & top each plate with 2 fried eggs. Serve immediately and enjoy.

Cauliflower and Feta Omelette

Prep Time: 10 minutes
Cooking Time: 15 minutes
Servings: 4

Ingredients

- 2 cups Cremini mushrooms, quartered or sliced
- 1 cup onion diced
- ¼ cup feta cheese, crumbled
- 3 garlic cloves, chopped
- ½ cup low- sodium vegetable or chicken stock
- 4 cups cauliflower rice, fresh or frozen
- 1 teaspoon dried thyme or 1 tablespoon fresh
- ¼ teaspoon black ground pepper
- 1 tablespoon olive oil
- ½ teaspoon salt

Directions

1. Over moderate heat in large skillet; heat the olive oil until hot.
2. Add in the onion and mushrooms, sauté for a couple of minutes, until the onions turn translucent.
3. Add in the garlic, cauliflower rice, pepper and salt.
4. Sauté for 3 to 5 minutes, until the cauliflower is tender slightly.
5. Add in the stock & thyme.
6. Continue cooking for 5 to 7 minutes, until cauliflower rice is completely tender & the liquid is almost absorbed.
7. Add in the feta; taste & adjust the amount of pepper, thyme & salt to preference.
8. Garnish with more of thyme & a bit more of feta, if desired. Serve immediately and enjoy.

Cauliflower Bread with Crispy Bacon, Poached Eggs & Avocado

Prep Time: 10 minutes
Cooking Time: 20 minutes
Servings: 2

Ingredients

- ½ – 1 tablespoon psyllium husk
- 2 cups cauliflower, grated
- ¼ spring onion, finely sliced
- 1-2 tablespoons coconut flour
- 4 large eggs
- ½ teaspoon garlic powder
- 3-4 bacon slices, organic, chemical-free, diced
- 1 avocado
- ½ teaspoon salt

Directions

1. Line two standard-sized baking trays with the baking paper and preheat your oven to 350 F in advance.
2. Combine 2 cups of grated cauliflower with 2 eggs, psyllium, 1 tablespoon coconut flour, garlic powder & salt. If the mixture seems to be too thin then add up to 1 tablespoon of flour to thicken, if required.
3. Split the cauliflower mix into two; placing each cauliflower blob onto one of the lined baking trays & shape the mixture into even rectangles using spatula or your hands; don't make them too thick or thin.
4. Place them in the preheated oven for 12 to 15 minutes.
5. Check the cauliflower toasts & rotate them in the oven. Bake until turn golden brown & cooked through, for 10 more minutes.
6. Add the bacon to the second baking tray & spread it out. Cook in the oven again until golden brown.
7. In the meantime; fill a small saucepan with water and bring it to a boil over moderate heat. Add a dash of apple cider vinegar & a pinch of salt.
8. When the water starts boiling, crack 2 eggs into the water to poach. Cook until the whites are completely cooked but the yolk is still running slightly.
9. Using a slotted spoon; remove & place them onto paper towels to remove any excess water.
10. When the cauliflower and bacon toasts are ready, start plating. Place the cauliflower toasts onto two plates and top them with the poached eggs, avocado, spring onion and crispy bacon.
11. Serve immediately and enjoy.

Cauliflower and Spinach Breakfast Bread

Prep Time: 10 minutes
Cooking Time: 20 minutes
Servings: 1 loaf

Ingredients

- 1 tablespoon pancetta
- ¾ cup plus 1 tablespoon almond flour
- 1 cup cauliflower rice (approximately ½ small cauliflower)
- ½ teaspoon baking soda
- 1 tablespoon butter or coconut oil, melted
- ½ teaspoon lemon juice
- 1 tablespoon jalapeño
- ½ teaspoon each of pepper & salt
- 1 large egg

Directions

1. Preheat your oven to 350 F in advance.
2. Cut half a head of the cauliflower into small chunks & place them in a food processor; pulse on high until the cauliflower resembles small grains and becomes uniform in size.
3. Combine cauliflower rice with almond flour, egg, lemon juice, baking soda, coconut oil, pepper & salt in a large bowl. Mix until combined well. Add in your favorite flavorings & make a ball form the dough.
4. Place the dough on a baking sheet lined with parchment paper; flatten slightly so the bread is roughly 1 ½" thick & place it in the oven
5. Bake until a toothpick comes out clean and turns golden in color, for 20 to 25 minutes. Keep an eye on the bread and ensure that you don't burn it.

Cauliflower Breakfast Muffins

Prep Time: 10 minutes
Cooking Time: 25 minutes
Servings: 9

Ingredients

- 1 ¼ cups diced ham
- 5 large eggs
- 1 ½ cups roughly chopped spinach
- ¼ teaspoon pepper
- 1 teaspoon mustard powder
- ¼ cup almond milk
- 1 ½ cups cauliflower rice, finely blended
- A pinch of cayenne
- ¼ teaspoon salt

Directions

1. Spray a standard-sized muffin tray with some cooking spray and preheat your oven to 350 F in advance.
2. Whisk the eggs with almond milk, mustard powder, pepper & salt in a large bowl; mix well and then add in the cauliflower rice.
3. Place a spoonful of the spinach and ham into the bottom of 9 muffin cups. Pour the cauliflower and egg mixture on top of each & then top each muffin with the leftover spinach and ham.
4. Bake in the preheated oven until the tops are completely set and the edges are browned lightly, for 20 to 25 minutes.
5. Run a spatula around each muffin to loosen & then arrange them on a wire rack to completely cool.

Cauliflower Pancakes

Prep Time: 10 minutes
Cooking Time: 30 minutes
Servings: 3

Ingredients

- 1 small head of cauliflower, trimmed & cut into florets
- ¼ teaspoon black pepper
- 2 tablespoons Parmesan, grated
- ½ cup part-skim mozzarella, shredded (approximately 2oz)
- 2 lightly beaten eggs, large
- ½ teaspoon garlic powder
- 3 tablespoons olive oil
- ½ teaspoon kosher salt

Directions

1. Line a large-sized baking sheet with the parchment paper and preheat your oven to 200 F in advance.
2. Place the cauliflower in a food processor & pulse until you get rice like consistency. If required, feel free to work in batches.
3. Combine the riced cauliflower with Parmesan, mozzarella, eggs, garlic powder, pepper and salt in a medium-sized bowl.
4. Over medium heat in a large skillet; heat 1 tablespoon of the oil until hot. Measure approximately ¼ measuring cup per pancake and place it in the hot skillet, flattening them thin using the back of a spoon. Fry the pancakes over medium heat until the underside has formed a sturdy, crust turns golden-brown, for 3 to 5 minutes.
5. Flip to the other side carefully & fry until both sides turn golden-brown & sturdy enough to lift off the skillet, 3 to 5 minutes more.
6. Repeat these steps for two more times. Before adding each batch; add a tablespoon of olive oil more. Keep the cooked cauliflower pancakes in the warm oven. Serve warm and enjoy.

Caramel Cauliflower Rice Frittata

Prep Time: 10 minutes
Cooking Time: 30 minutes
Servings: 4

Ingredients

- 4 large eggs
- 2 cups egg whites
- 1 large head cauliflower, broken into large pieces
- 2 tablespoons avocado oil
- A pinch each of garlic salt, ground black pepper, red pepper flakes & garlic powder or to taste

Directions

1. Set oven rack approximately 6" from the heat source & preheat your oven's broiler in advance.
2. Run the cauliflower through the food processor and create cauliflower "rice" using the shredding blade.
3. Now, over medium-high heat in an oven-safe skillet; heat the avocado oil. Add in the cauliflower "rice" & garlic salt; cook for a couple of minutes, until tender, stirring frequently.
4. Whisk eggs with egg whites, black pepper, garlic powder & salt in a large bowl; pour on top of the cauliflower mixture. Cook for 5 to 7 more minutes, until the eggs are almost set.
5. Place the skillet under the broiler for cook for 5 to 7 minutes, until the eggs are set completely. Let cool for 5 minutes. Serve and enjoy.

Appetizers & Sides

Cauliflower Pizza Crust

Prep Time: 15 minutes
Cooking Time: 15 minutes
Servings: 4

Ingredients

- 4 cups raw cauliflower rice (approximately one medium head)
- 1 teaspoon oregano, dried
- ⅓ cup goat cheese, soft
- 1 beaten egg, large
- A pinch of salt

Directions

1. Preheat your oven to 400 F in advance.
2. Work in batches and the raw cauliflower florets in a food processor, until you get rice like consistency.
3. Fill a large pot with approximately an inch of water; bring everything together to a boil. Add in the cauliflower "rice"; cover & let cook for 4 to 5 minutes. Drain into a fine-mesh strainer.
4. Once done, transfer it to a thin, clean dishtowel. Wrap up the steamed rice in the dishtowel, twist it up and then SQUEEZE out the moisture completely. Using your hands; combine the strained rice, goat cheese, beaten egg & spices in a large bowl.
5. Press the dough out onto a parchment paper lined baking sheet. Keep the dough approximately ⅓" thick & if desired, make the edges a little higher for a "crust" effect. Bake in the preheated oven for 35 to 40 minutes. When done; the crust should be firm & golden brown.
6. Add in your favorites such as cheese, sauce & any other toppings. Place the pizza back to the oven & bake until the cheese is just hot & bubbly, for 5 to 10 more minutes. Slice & serve immediately.

Cauliflower Soup

Prep Time: 15 minutes
Cooking Time: 50 minutes
Servings: 4

Ingredients

- 1 large head of cauliflower, broken into small florets, stems chopped
- 1 ½ cups vegetable stock or broth
- 1 yellow onion, medium, diced
- ½ teaspoon lemon zest
- 1 tablespoon fresh basil, chopped
- ½ cup un-oaked white wine
- 1 can light coconut milk (14 ounces)
- ¼ cup chives or green onions, chopped
- 1 to 3 teaspoons rice vinegar
- ½ teaspoon sugar
- 2 - 3 tablespoons Thai red curry paste
- Thinly sliced birds-eye peppers, jalapeño or Serrano, optional
- 4 tablespoons melted coconut oil or olive oil, divided
- Freshly ground black pepper and salt to taste

Directions

1. Preheat your oven to 400 F in advance. Toss the cauliflower with coconut oil enough to lightly coat the pieces. Spread the pieces on a large baking sheet in a single layer & roast for 25 to 30 minutes, until the tips are golden brown.
2. Now, over medium heat in a large, heavy-bottomed pot or Dutch oven, heat 1 tablespoon of coconut oil until it starts shimmering. Once done; immediately add the diced onion & a dash of salt; cook for a couple of minutes, until turns translucent, stirring every now and then. Add in the lemon zest and curry paste; give everything a good stir until well incorporated. Increase the heat to medium-high and then stir in the wine; cook until the wine has almost evaporated, stirring frequently.
3. Add the entire roasted cauliflower stems & half of the florets to the hot pot. Add in the coconut milk, vegetable broth & sugar. Stir well & bring the mixture to a gentle simmer, stirring every now and then. Continue to cook for 5 to 10 minutes more (maintain a gentle simmer throughout the cooking process). Remove the pot from heat; set aside and let cool for a couple of minutes. Blend the soup carefully using an immersion blender until completely smooth.
4. Stir in a teaspoon of vinegar, pepper and salt to taste. Feel free to stir in a few teaspoons of more vinegar, if you like your soup to be more acidity. Ladle the soup evenly into four bowls. Top each with approximately ¼ of the cauliflower florets, a sprinkle of freshly chopped basil, hot peppers and chives.

Carrot and Coriander Soup with Cauliflower Rice
Crumb

Prep Time: 10 minutes
Cooking Time: 20 minutes
Servings: 3

Ingredients

- 10 carrots, medium to large-sized (approximately 2 pounds)
- 1 ½ teaspoons ground coriander
- 1 celery stick, large
- 6 cups fresh stock (vegetable or chicken)
- Extra virgin olive oil
- 1 red onion, small
- Good pinch of cracked black pepper & salt

For the Crumb:

- Florets from ½ cauliflower
- Handful of fresh coriander, chopped
- Extra virgin olive oil
- Pepper & salt to taste

Directions

1. Fill a large pan with the stock and bring it to a boil over medium-high heat; let boil until the stock decreases by half, for 15 to 20 minutes.
2. Chop the carrots & celery and finely dice the onion.
3. Now, over moderate heat in a pan; heat a 1 tablespoon of olive oil until hot and then add in the onion, celery and carrots; cook until begin to soften, for 3 to 4 minutes.
4. Add the mixture to the stock with the dried coriander, a pinch of pepper and salt; cook for 12 to 15 more minutes. If required, feel free to add a small amount of more stock (ensure that the stock should cover the vegetables all the times).
5. In the meantime, prepare the cauliflower crumb. Remove the stalks from half a head of cauliflower & blitz in a food processor until you get rice like consistency.
6. Transfer to a steamer & cook until el dente, for 3 minutes. Set aside and let slightly cool. Transfer to a muslin cloth & squeeze any excess water out. Place it into the pan again & mix with 1 tablespoon of the melted coconut oil and then season with pepper and salt.
7. Once the vegetables are cooked, transfer them to a food processor or Vitamix and blitz until smooth. Feel free to add a small amount of more stock, if it's too thick. Pour your coriander and carrot soup into a bowl and top with the fresh coriander, cauliflower rice & a drizzle of extra virgin olive oil.

Curried Cauliflower Rice Kale Soup

Prep Time: 30 minutes
Cooking Time: 20 minutes
Servings: 4

Ingredients

- 5 to 6 cups of cauliflower florets (approximately 3 to 4 cups when "riced')
- 2- 3 tablespoon curry powder or curry seasoning (turmeric should be usually included in the curry seasoning/powder)
- ¼ teaspoon sea salt
- 1 teaspoon garlic powder
- ½ teaspoon paprika
- 2 cups carrots, chopped (5oz)
- ½ teaspoon cumin
- 2-3 tablespoon olive oil for roasting
- 1 teaspoon garlic, minced
- 8 kale leaves; stems removed & chopped
- ¾ cup red onion chopped
- 4 cups chicken or vegetable broth
- ½ teaspoon chili flakes or red pepper
- 1 cup coconut or almond milk
- ½ teaspoon black pepper
- 2 teaspoon avocado or olive oil
- Salt to taste

Directions

1. Preheat your oven to 400 F in advance.
2. Toss the cauliflower florets with the garlic powder, curry powder, paprika, cumin, 3 tablespoons of oil and salt in a small bowl.
3. Spread the cauliflower florets on a large-sized roasting pan or baking dish. Place in the preheated oven & roast until tender but ensure that these are not overcooked, for 20 to 22 minutes.
4. Remove from the oven & set aside at room temperature.
5. In the meantime, prepare your remaining veggies. Chop them up on a large-sized cutting board.
6. Place the cauliflower florets in a blender or Food Processor; pulse a couple of times until you get rice like consistency.
7. Once done and the veggies/kale are chopped, prepare your cooking pot.
8. Now, over moderate heat in a large stock pot; heat 2 teaspoon of oil until hot. Once done add in the onion & minced garlic. Sautee until fragrant, for 3 to 5 minutes.
9. Add in the broth, cauliflower "rice," veggies, milk, red chili pepper & black pepper.
10. Bring everything together to a quick boil and then let simmer until the veggies are cooked through, for 20 more minutes.
11. Once ready to serve; feel free to add a dash of sea salt, if desired.
12. Garnish with nut/seed crackers crumbles and herbs.

Cauliflower Chowder

Prep Time: 10 minutes
Cooking Time: 30 minutes
Servings: 6

Ingredients

- 2 cups canned coconut milk, full fat
- 1 boneless skinless chicken breast
- 2 stalks celery, diced
- 1 onion, small, chopped
- 2 cups cauliflower rice
- ¼ cup fresh flat-leaf parsley
- 2 carrots, peeled and diced
- 1 teaspoon fresh thyme
- 4 cups chicken stock, or broth
- 1 bay leaf
- 2 tablespoons olive oil or ghee
- Pepper & salt

Directions

1. Over moderate heat in a large soup pot; heat the ghee until completely melted. Once done; add in the onion, celery and carrot. Cook until the vegetables start to turn soften; for 5 to 8 minutes. Stir in the thyme and then season with pepper and salt.
2. Pour in the chicken stock & add the bay leaf. Bring everything together to a boil. Once done; immediately decrease the heat to a low simmer. Add in the chicken breast. Cover & let simmer until the chicken is cooked through, for 12 to 15 minutes.
3. Remove the chicken from pot & separate it into shreds using two forks. Discard the bay leaf.
4. Place the shredded chicken back to the pot along with the cauliflower rice. Let simmer until the cauliflower is cooked, for 3 to 5 more minutes. Stir in the coconut milk & parsley; cook for a couple of minutes, until warmed through. Season with pepper and salt to taste.

Cauliflower Tabbouleh Salad

Prep Time: 55 minutes
Cooking Time: 10 minutes
Servings: 2

Ingredients

- 1 avocado
- 1 cup cauliflower rice
- Two ⅛" slices of Jicama
- 1 Persian cucumber, diced
- 1 tablespoon olive oil
- Juice from ¼ lemon
- 1 teaspoon Brain Octane Oil
- 1 cup parsley
- ½ teaspoon sea salt

Directions

1. Over medium heat in a large skillet; heat two tablespoons of water & then add the rice cauliflower. Cover & cook for 2 minutes. Remove from heat; set aside and let cool for 3 to 5 minutes.
2. Add parsley to a food processor & blend until chopped finely.
3. Add cauliflower rice to the food processor & blend until chopped finely & then combine it with the parsley.
4. Add cucumber with parsley and cauliflower to a large-sized mixing bowl.
5. Add in the olive oil, Brain Octane, lemon juice and salt into the mixing bowl; thoroughly mix & refrigerate for an hour.
6. Add jicama slices to a large plate. Mash the avocado into a smooth paste & evenly spread over the jicama.
7. Top the jicama slices with the tabbouleh mixture; serve & enjoy.

Italian Roasted Cauliflower Salad

Prep Time: 15 minutes
Cooking Time: 10 minutes
Servings: 5

Ingredients

- 2½ cup rice cauliflower
- 1 teaspoon Italian seasoning
- ¼ cup sun dried tomatoes
- 3 tablespoons dried basil or ½ bunch or 1 cups of fresh basil, chopped
- ¼ cup pine nuts
- 2 tablespoons balsamic vinegar
- ½ cup cherry tomatoes, sliced
- 1 tablespoon lemon juice, freshly squeezed
- ¼ cup Burrata cheese, optional
- 1½ teaspoon salt

Directions

1. Process the head of a cauliflower in a food processor until you get rice like consistency. Now, toss the entire ingredients together in a large bowl.
2. Let chill & serve.

Roasted Cauliflower with Avocado Lime Cilantro Dressing

Prep Time: 10 minutes
Cooking Time: 30 minutes
Servings: 4

Ingredients

- 1 head cauliflower
- Olive oil
- Salt to taste

For the Dressing

- 1 garlic clove
- Juice of 1 lime, freshly squeezed
- 1 small handful of fresh cilantro
- 4 tablespoon water
- 1 avocado
- 2 tablespoon olive oil
- Pepper & salt, to taste

For Toppings

- Sunflower seeds
- Roughly chopped cilantro, fresh

Directions

1. Preheat your oven to 425 F in advance.
2. Remove stem & leaves from cauliflower. Cut the head into smaller pieces and then place them in a large bowl. Drizzle with a tablespoon of olive oil & then sprinkle with salt to taste; toss well.
3. Spread the cauliflower pieces on a large-sized baking tray in a single layer & roast in the preheated oven for 30 minutes, flipping & rotating the pieces halfway during the cooking process.
4. In the meantime, prepare the dressing. Place the entire ingredients together in a blender; blend on high until completely combined & creamy. Feel free to add more of water, if desired.
5. Remove cauliflower from oven; once it's golden.. Drizzle the dressing on top of the cauliflower pieces. Sprinkle with roughly chopped cilantro & sunflower seeds. Serve immediately and enjoy.

Indian Cauliflower Fried Rice with Roasted Chickpeas

Prep Time: 15 minutes
Cooking Time: 30 minutes
Servings: 4

Ingredients

For Roasted Chickpeas
- 1 cup chickpeas drained
- 1 teaspoon garlic powder
- ½ teaspoon pepper or to taste
- 1 teaspoon smoked paprika
- ¼ teaspoon salt or to taste
- 1 teaspoon cumin

For Indian Cauliflower Fried Rice with Chicken
- 1 teaspoon cumin ground
- 2 boneless and skinless chicken breasts, cut into 1" cubes
- 1 large cauliflower; broken into florets
- ¼ teaspoon cayenne pepper
- 1 teaspoon garam masala
- ½ teaspoon ground turmeric
- 2 garlic cloves, minced
- 1 teaspoon grated ginger, fresh
- 2 tablespoons cilantro for garnish
- 1 cup frozen peas
- 2 tablespoon olive oil
- 1 small onion chopped
- ½ teaspoon salt
- 1 cup shredded carrots

Directions

1. Lightly coat a large-sized baking sheet with the cooking spray and preheat your oven to 400 F in advance.
2. Toss the chickpeas with the garlic powder, cumin, smoked paprika, pepper and salt in a medium bowl. Toss well until nicely coated. Spread the chickpeas over the prepared baking sheet in an even layer.
3. Roast in the preheated oven until dry & crispy on the outside, for 20 to 30 minutes.
4. In the meantime; work in batches & place the cauliflower florets in a food processor; pulse on high until you get rice like consistency. Place in a large bowl & set aside.
5. Combine cumin with cayenne pepper, garam masala, turmeric and salt in a medium bowl. Add the chicken pieces; toss well.
6. Now, heat 1 tablespoon of olive oil over medium high heat in a large skillet or wok. Add in the minced garlic & ginger; cook for a couple of seconds. Add chicken to the wok & cook until the chicken starts to brown a bit and is no longer pink, for 5 to 6 minutes, stirring frequently to prevent burning.
7. Remove the chicken from the wok and then add the leftover olive oil. Add onion, peas and carrots. Cook & stir for a couple of minutes. Add in the cauliflower rice; stir well and then cook until cauliflower is tender, for 4 more minutes. Season with pepper and salt, if required. Place the chicken back to the wok & heat through.
8. Serve warm topped with the roasted chickpeas & cilantro.

Honey Lime Sriracha Glazed Cauliflower Wings

Prep Time: 15 minutes
Cooking Time: 25 minutes
Servings: 4

Ingredients

- 4 cups of cauliflower florets (roughly 1 head)
- 1 cup milk or water or almond milk
- ½ cup gluten-free rice flour or all-purpose flour
- 1 cup panko breadcrumbs
- 2 teaspoon garlic powder
- 1 teaspoon cumin
- ¼ teaspoon ground pepper
- 1 teaspoon paprika or chili powder
- ¼ teaspoon salt

For the Sauce:

- ¼ cup sriracha
- ⅓ cup honey
- 1 tablespoon sesame seeds
- ¼ cup ketchup

Directions

1. Place a piece of parchment paper on two baking sheets, set aside. Position a rack in the middle of your oven & preheat the oven to 400 F in advance.
2. Wash & cut the cauliflower head into small florets or bite sized pieces. Place the Panko breadcrumbs in a large-sized shallow bowl.
3. Mix the flour/milk/water & spices in a medium-sized mixing bowl. Work in batches and dip the cauliflower first into the batter; shaking off any excess batter and then dip into the panko breadcrumbs.
4. Lay the cauliflower on the baking sheet in a single layer. Drizzle with oil olive & bake until the crust is crispy & golden, for 20 to 25 minutes.
5. Whisk the ketchup with honey and sriracha in a large bowl. Remove the wings from oven & toss them in the sriracha-honey sauce; sprinkle some sesame seeds over the top. Serve with ranch sauce or blue cheese and enjoy.

Buffalo Cauliflower Bites

Prep Time: 10 minutes
Cooking Time: 30 minutes
Servings: 4 persons

Ingredients

- ½ cup brown rice flour
- 1 head cauliflower; chopped into bite size piece
- A pinch each of granulated garlic powder & kosher salt
- ½ cup water
- Non-stick spray

For Sauce:
- 1 teaspoon melted butter substitute such as Earth Balance
- ½ cup Frank's Red Hot sauce

Directions

1. Preheat your oven to 450 F in advance.
2. Combine brown rice flour with garlic powder, water & salt in a small bowl. Thoroughly mix with a whisk. Dip the cauliflower pieces in the prepared batter until evenly coated and then arrange them on a non-stick baking sheet, lightly greased.
3. Bake in the preheated oven until the batter hardens, for 8 to 10 minutes; flip with a spatula & bake for 5 more minutes.
4. Whisk the Hot sauce with Earth Balance in a small bowl. When the cauliflower is done; evenly brush each piece with the hot sauce mixture using a plastic pastry brush.
5. Bake the coated cauliflower until sauce looks absorbed and cauliflower is crispy, for 8 to 10 more minutes. Remove from oven; set aside & let rest for 20 minutes. Serve and enjoy.

Cauliflower Rice Maki Rolls

Prep Time: 30 minutes
Cooking Time: 15 minutes
Servings: 8 persons

Ingredients

- 1 pound raw sushi fish, fresh (tuna, salmon or even white fish)
- 2 heads cauliflower; riced
- 1 large Avocado
- 4 tablespoon rice vinegar
- 1 organic cucumber, small
- 8 sheets of Nori Seaweed
- 1 ½ cup cream cheese
- 2 tablespoon sugar
- ½ ripe mango
- 2 tablespoon chili mayo

To Serve
- Pickled ginger
- Wasabi paste
- Edamame beans in pods, steamed and sprinkled with salt and lime juice
- Soya
- Wakame, marinated seaweed salad

Directions

1. Fill a large pot with water (enough to cover the riced cauliflower) and boil the cauliflower rice for a couple of minutes. Strain well and then pour some cold water over them until it cools down, let any excess water to drain. Wrap the cauliflower rice completely in a dishtowel & squeeze the entire water from the cauliflower. Now, combine the cauliflower rice with rice vinegar, cream cheese & sugar in a large bowl.
2. Cut the mango, vegetables & fish into suiting long & slim pieces. Place a piece of nori (rough side facing upwards) over the bamboo mat. Add a few tablespoons of the cauliflower rice; evenly divide over the nori sheet (leaving approximately ½ to 1 cm free in the top). Place the filling in a straight slim line into the bottom part of the nori sheet.
3. Then tuck in the filling using your hands on the bamboo mat, rolling up around half of the roll & gently press it firm. Keep using the bamboo mat to gently roll up the rest of the maki roll and 'close' it by adding a little water on the free tip of nori weed and roll it all the way up.
4. Store the maki rolls in a fridge until ready to eat. When ready; cut them roughly into 2 ½ cm to 1" pieces & serve them along with your favorite sushi accessories.

Cauliflower Mushroom Risotto

Prep Time: 20 minutes
Cooking Time: 20 minutes
Servings: 4

Ingredients

- 1 large head of cauliflower, cut into small florets
- ½ cup beef stock
- 1 yellow onion, large, diced
- ¾ pound mushrooms, sliced thinly
- 2 garlic cloves, large, minced
- Fresh parsley, chopped
- 1 tablespoon coconut oil
- Pepper and salt, to taste

Directions

1. Wash the cauliflower florets & then place them on paper towels to dry.
2. Work in batches & process the cauliflower florets in a blender or food processor until you get rice like consistency.
3. Now, over medium heat in a large skillet; heat the coconut oil & sauté the onions for a couple of minutes, until tender & caramelized. Add in the garlic; give everything a good stir and cook for a couple of more minutes, until fragrant. Add in the mushrooms & continue to sauté until brown on both sides.
4. Add in the cauliflower rice & beef stock; decrease the heat to low. Continue to cook the cauliflower rice for 10 more minutes, until it absorbs the beef stock and is tender but not mushy.
5. Add pepper and salt to taste. Garnish with fresh chopped parsley. Evenly divide the mixture among the bowls. Serve and enjoy.

Cauliflower Fried Rice

Prep Time: 30 minutes
Cooking Time: 30 minutes
Servings: 4 persons

Ingredients

- 1 organic egg, large
- 2 egg whites
- 1 medium head of cauliflower, rinsed; core removed & dry
- 2 cloves garlic, minced
- ½ small onion, finely diced
- 5 scallions, diced; greens & whites separated
- ½ cup peas & carrots, frozen
- 3 tablespoon soy sauce or to taste (Coconut aminos for Paleo or Tamari for gluten-free)
- Cooking spray
- 1 tablespoon sesame oil
- A pinch of salt

Directions

1. Coarsely chop the cauliflower into small florets; place half of the cauliflower florets into a food processor & pulse for a minute or two, until you get rice like consistency (ensure that you don't over process). Set aside & repeat this step with the leftover cauliflower florets as well.
2. Combine egg with egg whites in a small-sized bowl; beat well using a large fork and then season with salt to taste.
3. Now, coat a large wok or sauté pan with the oil and heat it over medium heat.
4. Add in the eggs & cook until set, turning a couple of times; set aside.
5. Add in the sesame oil & sauté the onions with scallion whites, carrots, peas & garlic until soft, for 3 to 5 minutes. Increase the heat to medium-high.
6. Add in the cauliflower "rice" along with the soy sauce to the sauté pan. Mix well; cover & cook until the cauliflower is crispy slightly on the outside but still tender on the inside, for a couple of more minutes, stirring every now and then.
7. Add egg; immediately remove the sauté pan from the heat source & then mix in scallion greens. Serve and enjoy.

Cajun Cauliflower Rice

Prep Time: 10 minutes
Cooking Time: 15 minutes
Servings: 4 persons

Ingredients

- 2 Turkey Andouille Sausage Links
- 4 cups riced cauliflower or approximately ½ head of cauliflower
- 2 garlic cloves, minced
- ½ cup white or yellow onion, finely chopped
- 2 tablespoon ghee or butter
- ½ cup green bell peppers, finely chopped
- 4 green onions, thinly sliced (both white and green parts)
- 2 tablespoon vegetable or olive oil

For Seasonings Mixture:
- ¼ teaspoon dried thyme
- ½ teaspoon black pepper
- ¼ teaspoon ground mustard
- ¾ teaspoon paprika
- ¼ teaspoon cayenne or more, to taste
- ½ teaspoon cumin
- ¼ teaspoon dried oregano
- ½ teaspoon salt

Directions

1. Combine the entire seasonings ingredients together into a small-sized bowl; mix well & set the mixture aside.
2. Cut the cauliflower into very small florets and then place them into a food processor. Work in batches & pulse for a minute or two, until you get "rice" like consistency. Set them aside.
3. Now, over medium-high heat in a large skillet; heat 2 tablespoon of oil. Add in the chopped white onion, green pepper and garlic. Sauté for a couple of minutes.
4. Dice up the sausages in advance. Add them into the skillet with the peppers and onions and then add in the green onions. Continue to sauté for 2 minutes more.
5. Add 2 tablespoon of butter or ghee & let melt; add in the riced cauliflower & the seasonings mixture. Continue to sauté for 2 to 4 minutes more.
6. Serve immediately & enjoy.

Cauliflower Rice Turkey Stuffing

Prep Time: 20 minutes
Cooking Time: 30 minutes
Servings: 8

Ingredients

- ½ pound cremini mushrooms, sliced
- 1 pound ground pork or sweet Italian sausage
- 2 celery stalks, chopped
- 1 small onion, chopped
- 3 carrots, chopped
- 1 cup parsnips chopped
- 2 teaspoon thyme, minced
- 1 shallot, chopped
- ½ cup dried currants
- 6 cup cauliflower rice
- 1 leek, thinly sliced (only white portion)
- 1-2 tablespoon turkey drippings
- 1 teaspoon rosemary, minced
- 2 cup collard greens, thinly shredded
- 1 Portobello mushroom, cubed
- ½ cup almonds, sliced
- 4 tablespoon ghee or butter
- Pepper & salt to taste

Directions

1. Over medium high heat in a large cast iron skillet; heat ghee or butter until completely melted.
2. Add in the sweet Italian sausage & cook until cooked through.
3. Once done, remove the meat & set it aside
4. Add onions with celery, carrots, parsnips and leek in the same skillet. Feel free to add more of oil, if required.
5. Continue to cook until the vegetable turn tender and then add in the rosemary and thyme; toss well.
6. Cook for 3 more minutes & then remove it from the heat.
7. In the meantime, over medium heat in a separate pan; heat 1 tablespoon of ghee or butter.
8. Once hot; add and cook the mushrooms. Sprinkle salt over the mushrooms & set aside
9. Add 2 tablespoons of ghee or butter in a very large pan and heat it over moderate heat.
10. Once hot, immediately add and cook the shallot for a minute or two, until soft.
11. Add in the cauliflower rice; toss well until evenly combined.
12. Add 1 tablespoon of the turkey dripping & toss again; sprinkle with salt to taste
13. Add in the collard greens & toss well.
14. Cook for a couple of more minutes, until the cauliflower has softened but ensure that it's not soggy.
15. Once the cauliflower is ready; immediately add in the entire cooked components of the dish (vegetable/onion mix & mushrooms); toss well until evenly combined
16. Serve with sliced almonds and currants on top.

Asian Cauliflower Rice Lettuce Cups

Prep Time: 20 minutes
Cooking Time: 35 minutes
Servings: 4

Ingredients

- Farro (½ of an 8-ounce package), cooked as per the directions
- 3 tablespoon Ginger Stir-In Paste
- 1 pkg cauliflower rice (1 pound)
- 2 tablespoon sesame oil
- 1 head bok choy (approximately ¼ pound), trimmed, sliced thinly
- 2 tablespoon Mirin Sweet Cooking Rice Seasoning
- ½ cup matchstick carrots, organic
- A bunch of green onions, trimmed & sliced thinly
- 1 tablespoon roasted salted whole cashews, chopped, for garnish
- 2 tablespoon Asian Classics Soy Sauce
- Szechuan Chili garlic sauce to taste
- 2 tablespoon vegetable oil
- 1 package green lettuce leaves, fresh (7 oz)
- Salt to taste

Directions

1. Over high heat in a stir-fry pan; heat the vegetable oil. Once hot; add & cook the faro, until browned, for 3 to 4 minutes, stirring frequently.
2. Add in the bok choy and cauliflower; cook for a minute or two more, stirring frequently. Add in the garlic, ginger & carrots; continue to cook for a minute more, stirring frequently.
3. Add in the sesame oil, mirin, soy sauce & green onions; give everything a good stir until evenly combined. Cook for 2 to 3 more minutes, stirring frequently. Season with salt to taste.
4. Arrange the lettuce leaves on clean, large-sized serving platter; evenly divide the farro mixture over the leaves. Garnish with chopped cashews and drizzle with the Szechuan Sauce. Serve and enjoy.

Creamy Mashed Cauliflower

Prep Time: 15 minutes
Cooking Time: 15 minutes
Servings: 4 persons

Ingredients

- 1 garlic clove, smashed
- 1 head cauliflower, cut into florets
- ¼ cup Parmesan cheese, grated
- 1 tablespoon cream cheese, low-fat
- ⅛ teaspoon freshly ground black pepper
- 1 tablespoon olive oil
- ½ teaspoon kosher salt

Directions

1. Fill a saucepan with water (just below the bottom of the steamer) and then place a steamer insert into it. Bring it to a boil over moderate heat. Once done; add in the cauliflower; cover & let steam for 8 to 10 minutes, until tender.
2. In the meantime, over medium heat in a small skillet; heat the olive oil; cook & stir the garlic for 2 minutes, until softened. Immediately remove it from the heat.
3. Transfer ½ of the cauliflower into a food processor; cover & blend on high until you get rice like consistency. Slowly add in the leftover cauliflower florets and continue to blend, until the vegetables are creamy. Blend in the Parmesan cheese, garlic, cream cheese, black pepper & salt.

Crispy Orange Cauliflower

Prep Time: 10 minutes
Cooking Time: 25 minutes
Servings: 8 persons

Ingredients

For the Soy-Orange Sauce:
- 3 garlic cloves, minced
- ¼ teaspoon ginger powder
- 1 tablespoon soy sauce or tamari, low-sodium
- ½ teaspoon cornstarch
- 1 tablespoon rice vinegar
- ½ cup orange juice, pulp-free
- 4 teaspoons honey (or pure maple syrup)
- ½ teaspoon sesame oil
- 1 tablespoon cold water
- ¼ teaspoon hot pepper flakes

For the Stir-Fry
- 1 head cauliflower, grated/minced
- 15.7 ounces Gorton's smart & crunchy fish sticks
- 4 ½ ounces carrots, diced (roughly 2 medium)
- ½ teaspoon ginger
- 6 green onions, sliced thinly
- 3 organic eggs, large
- 1½ cups sweet peas, frozen
- 3 garlic cloves, minced
- 4 tablespoons soy sauce or tamari, low-sodium
- 3 tablespoons sesame oil

Directions

For the Soy-Orange Sauce:
1. Over moderate heat in a small pot; heat the sesame oil until hot and then sauté the garlic for a minute or two, then stir in the rice vinegar, orange juice, tamari or soy sauce, ginger powder, honey & hot pepper flakes; bring everything together to a simmer.
2. Combine cornstarch with cold water in a small bowl & prepare a slurry. Whisk the cornstarch into the sauce & let simmer until thickened, for 5 to 7 minutes.
3. Remove & set aside.

For the Stir Fry:
1. Preheat your oven to 375 F in advance and then bake the Fish Sticks as per the instructions (flipping halfway during the baking time).
2. In the meantime, heat 1 tablespoon of the sesame oil over moderate heat in a large sauté pan & scramble three eggs. Transfer the eggs to a large bowl & set aside, then wipe the pan clean.
3. Add two tablespoons more of sesame oil to the hot pan & heat it medium-high heat.
4. Add in the minced garlic & cook for a minute. Add in the diced carrots & cook for 2 to 3 more minutes. Add in the sliced green onions & powdered ginger; cook for a minute.
5. Add in the riced cauliflower & cook for 4 minutes, stirring every now and then.
6. Add in the tamari or soy sauce & peas; cook for a minute. Put the pot with the soy-orange sauce over medium-high heat again. If required, feel free to use a splash of orange juice to thin.
7. Fold in the scrambled egg & plate the cauliflower fried rice. Top each plate with fish sticks & prepared orange- soy sauce; serve warm & enjoy.

Paella with Cauliflower Rice

Prep Time: 30 minutes
Cooking Time: 30 minutes
Servings: 4 persons

Ingredients

- ½ pound shrimp, deveined (and peeled if desired)
- 1 large cauliflower
- ¼ pound ham, diced
- 1 onion, diced
- 4 garlic cloves, minced
- 1 teaspoon paprika
- ¼ cup dry white wine
- 1 teaspoon turmeric or 2 pinches of saffron threads
- Zest & juice of ½ lemon
- ¼ cup paella broth, or chicken or fish stock
- 1 red bell pepper (reserve approximately ¼ cup), diced
- 2 Spanish chorizo sausages, sliced
- 1 yellow or orange bell pepper, diced
- Lemon slices, fresh for garnish
- 2 tablespoons olive oil
- ¼ cup parsley, chopped

For Spicy Garlic Finishing Sauce
- 4 garlic cloves
- ½ teaspoon cumin
- 1 jalapeno, ribs & seeds removed, chopped roughly
- ¼ cup red pepper, diced
- 1 teaspoon turmeric
- ¼ teaspoon pepper to taste
- ½ cup extra virgin olive oil
- ¼ cup parsley, divided
- ½ teaspoon salt

Directions

1. Cut cauliflower into small florets & then pulse them in a food processor for a minute, until you get rice or couscous like consistency; set aside.
2. Now, over medium high heat in a large, deep skillet; heat the oil until hot. Add and sauté the onion for a couple of minutes, until softened, then add in the garlic and bell pepper. Cook for a couple of minutes, until turn golden browned lightly. Stir in the cauliflower and then add in the spices, paella base or stock & white wine. Stir in the chorizo & ham; sauté for 5 more minutes, stirring every now and then.
3. Add in the shrimp & parsley; cook for a couple of more minutes, until the shrimp is cooked through.
4. Drizzle with a small amount of lemon juice & place lemon's slices on top.
5. Serve; drizzled with the finishing sauce. Serve with lemon slices on each plate and enjoy.

For Spicy Garlic Finishing Sauce

1. Blend the entire sauce ingredients (except half of the parsley) together in a high-power blender. Stir in the parsley & drizzle on top of the paella.

Roasted Sweet Potato and Cauliflower Rice Collard Wraps

Prep Time: 15 minutes
Cooking Time: 15 minutes
Servings: 4 servings

Ingredients

For the Collard Wraps:
- 1-⅓ to 2 cups cauliflower rice or Thai Cauliflower Rice
- 1 avocado, ripe, peeled & sliced
- 4 collard leaves, trimmed & shaved
- 1 sweet potato, large, roasted & mashed

For Almond Butter Ginger Sauce:
- ¼ cup creamy unsweetened almond butter, unsalted
- 1 tablespoon lime juice, freshly squeezed
- 2 teaspoons pure maple syrup
- 1 tablespoon ginger, fresh, peeled & grated
- ⅓ cup plus 1 tablespoon light coconut milk
- A pinch of sea salt

Directions

1. Whisk the entire ingredients for Almond Butter Ginger Sauce together in a small bowl until thick, creamy & combined well. Set aside at room temperature until ready to use.
2. In the meantime; chop the rough stem from the collard leaves off and shaving it down.
3. Add your desired amount of mashed sweet potato to the middle of each leaf, followed by approximately ⅓ to ½ cup of the cauliflower rice & sliced avocado.
4. Fold in the edges of collard leaf, creating a burrito. Using a sharp knife; carefully slice in half & serve with the prepared almond butter-ginger sauce. Enjoy.

Green Chile Cauliflower Casserole

Prep Time: 10 minutes
Cooking Time: 30 minutes
Servings: 6

Ingredients

- 1 cup sharp cheddar, shredded
- ¾ cup onion, chopped
- 2 cups cauliflower rice, frozen
- ½ teaspoon granulated garlic
- 1 cup Monterrey Jack cheese, shredded
- ½ cup full-fat sour cream
- 4 ounces green chiles, canned, drained
- ½ cup heavy cream
- 2 tablespoon butter
- ½ teaspoon black pepper
- 1 ½ teaspoon salt
- ¾ cup celery, chopped

Directions

1. Lightly grease or butter an 8x8" pan; set aside and preheat your oven to 325 F in advance.
2. Cook the frozen cauliflower rice as per the directions mentioned on the package or steam the cauliflower rice until slightly tender, for 3 to 4 minutes, if using fresh. Remove the steamed cauliflower rice from heat source; set aside until easy to handle & then squeeze to remove the excess moisture (ensure that it's fairly dry and not watery); set aside until ready to use.
3. Now, over medium high heat in a medium-sized sauté pan; heat the butter until melted. Add onions and celery; cook until tender, for 5 to 7 minutes. Decrease the heat to medium & add in the cream; continue to stir until thick, creamy and decreases by half; set aside.
4. Combine the cauliflower rice with ½ cup of each cheese, sour cream, chiles, veggie mixture & seasonings in a large bowl; give everything a good stir until well incorporated. Evenly spread the mixture in the prepared pan & top with the leftover cheese. Bake in the preheated oven until bubbly, for 20 to 25 minutes. Serve immediately & enjoy.

Mexican Cauliflower Rice

Prep Time: 15 minutes
Cooking Time: 15 minutes
Servings: 3

Ingredients

- 3 cups cauliflower florets; remove the stems & washed
- 1 jalapeno, chopped finely
- 3-4 garlic cloves, minced
- 1 small onion, chopped finely
- 2 medium tomatoes, chopped finely
- ½ teaspoon red chili powder or paprika powder
- 1 teaspoon cumin powder
- ¾ cup bell peppers, diced
- 1 tablespoon cilantro or coriander, chopped
- More of sliced avocados, cilantro, lime juice, or jalapenos for topping
- 1 tablespoon olive oil
- Salt to taste

Directions

1. Add cauliflower florets to a chopper or food processor; pulse for half a minute to a minute, until you get rice like consistency.
2. Now, over moderate heat in a large pan; heat the oil until hot & then add in the onions, jalapenos and garlic. Stir fry until the garlic is fragrant and the onion is translucent, for a couple of minutes.
3. Add in the tomatoes, paprika powder, cumin powder & salt to the pan. Cook until they soften, for a few more minutes. Add in the cauliflower rice and diced bell peppers to the pan; mix well. Continue to stir-fry until tender, for 3 to 4 more minutes.
4. Top with your favorite topping; serve hot & enjoy.

Cabbage Roll Skillet Casserole

Prep Time: 15 minutes
Cooking Time: 25 minutes
Servings: 4 persons

Ingredients

- 1 ½ pounds hamburger
- ½ cup ketchup
- 1 whole onion, chopped
- 8 oz. tomato sauce
- 1 ½ cup cauliflower rice
- 1 can diced tomatoes (15 oz.)
- 2 teaspoons Montreal Steak Seasoning
- 1 cabbage, medium, chopped
- ¼ to ½ teaspoon red peppers
- 1 teaspoon coarse black pepper
- ½ teaspoon salt

Directions

1. Over medium heat in a large skillet; brown the hamburger. Add onion, steak seasoning, pepper & salt; give everything a good stir until the ingredients are combined well.
2. Add in the cabbage, cauliflower rice and tomato sauce, ketchup and diced tomatoes.
3. Decrease the heat to low and let simmer until the cabbage turns tender, for a couple of minutes, stirring every now and then. Serve hot & enjoy.

Low Carb Keto Cheesy Cheddar Cauliflower Rice

Prep Time: 5 minutes
Cooking Time: 5 minutes
Servings: 6 persons

Ingredients

- 4 slices no sugar bacon, cooked, crisp & chopped
- ½ cup cheddar cheese, shredded or chopped
- 1 head cauliflower, pulse in a food processor until riced
- ¼ teaspoon garlic powder
- 2 ounces cream cheese
- ¼ teaspoon salt, optional

Directions

1. Place the riced cauliflower in a microwavable dish; cover & cook in the microwave for upto five minutes on high power.
2. Add in the cheese; stir until completely melted.
3. Stir in the leftover ingredients. Serve and enjoy.

Cauliflower Bacon Fritters

Prep Time: 15 minutes
Cooking Time: 15 minutes
Servings: 4 persons

Ingredients

- ½ teaspoon garlic powder
- 4 cups cauliflower rice
- ½ cup tapioca flour
- 3 organic eggs, large
- ½ teaspoon oregano
- 1 cup carrots, shredded
- 2 teaspoons apple cider vinegar
- ¼ cup white onion, diced
- 1 teaspoon salt-free chili powder
- ¼ cup nutritional yeast
- 2 teaspoons pink Himalayan salt

Directions

1. Line a large-sized baking sheet pan with the parchment paper and preheat your oven to 400 F in advance.
2. Whisk the eggs together in a small bowl. Add cauliflower rice with apple cider vinegar, tapioca flour, shredded carrots, onion, pink chili powder, Himalayan salt, nutritional yeast, garlic powder, eggs and oregano in a large-sized mixing bowl. Mix together until completely combined.
3. Make 8 patties from the batter using your hands (make a ball and then pat down on the prepared baking sheet & squeeze the sides in).
4. Bake in the preheated oven for 20 minutes; flip the patty carefully & slightly press the top down. Bake until crisp, for 10 to 15 more minutes.
5. Serve immediately with your favorite dip or a side of ketchup.

Baked Cauliflower Tater Tots

Prep Time: 25 minutes
Cooking Time: 40 minutes
Servings: 6 persons

Ingredients

- 3 cups cauliflower, cut into bite-sized florets
- 1 ½ cups almond meal
- 1 large egg white
- 3 tablespoon parsley, minced
- 1 ½ tablespoon minced garlic, fresh
- 3 tablespoon tapioca starch*
- ½ cup onion, diced
- 4 teaspoon coconut flour
- Olive oil spray
- 1 tablespoon extra-virgin olive oil
- A generous pinch of pepper
- ½ teaspoon sea salt

Directions

1. Line a large-sized baking sheet with the parchment paper and preheat your oven to 400 F in advance.
2. Place the cauliflower florets in a large food processor; process on high until you get "rice" like consistency. Transfer to a large, microwave-safe bowl & cook in the preheated oven for 3 minutes. Stir well & cook for 2 minutes more.
3. Add onion with garlic, parsley, pepper and salt into the bowl; stir well. Then, add in the egg white; stir until combined well. Finally, add the olive oil; stir well.
4. Add the coconut flour, almond meal and tapioca to the bowl; give everything a good stir until the cauliflower mixture thickens & mixed well.
5. Pack the cauliflower into a 1 tablespoon measuring spoon & hit it into your hand lightly until the cauliflower comes out in a perfect "tot" shape. Arrange the prepared tots over the baking sheet.
6. Generously spray the tops with olive oil spray & bake for 20 to 25 more minutes. Flip & generously spray with the spray again. Bake until turn crispy & golden brown, for 8 to 10 more minutes.
7. Serve immediately & enjoy.

Cauliflower Mac and Cheese

Prep Time: 2 minutes
Cooking Time: 5 minutes
Servings: 2 persons

Ingredients

- 1 ounce cheddar cheese shredded
- ¾ cup cauliflower florets, fresh or frozen with a small amount of water
- 1 tablespoon heavy cream

Directions

1. Dish a small microwavable with lid, microwave the cauliflower for a minute, covered.
2. Remove & chop the cauliflower into small pieces.
3. Microwave for 50 more seconds and then add in the shredded cheese.
4. Microwave for 10 seconds more.
5. Stir in the melted cheese and then stir in the heavy cream until sauce forms.
6. Serve immediately & enjoy.

Entrees

Cauliflower Rice Tortillas

Prep Time: 15 minutes
Cooking Time: 15 minutes
Servings: 4

Ingredients

- 2 organic eggs, large
- A head of cauliflower, stems removed & cut up
- ½ teaspoon paprika
- Freshly ground black pepper & sea salt to taste
- ½ teaspoon dried oregano

Directions

1. Preheat your oven to 375 F in advance.
2. Add the cauliflower florets into a food processor or blender and process on high until you get rice like consistency.
3. Steam the riced cauliflower over boiling water for a couple of minutes. Set aside and let cool at room temperature until easy to handle.
4. Once done; place the steamed cauliflower in a large-sized dish towel & squeeze the water out as much as you can.
5. Transfer the dried cauliflower to a large bowl. Add eggs with paprika, oregano & then season to taste.
6. Make six even-sized balls from the mixture & spread each ball out on a baking sheet lined with parchment paper.
7. Place in the preheated oven & bake for 8 to 10 minutes; carefully flip & cook the other side for 5 more minutes.
8. When ready to serve; reheat in a pan set over low heat.

Spanish Chicken with Cauliflower Rice

Prep Time: 10 minutes
Cooking Time: 20 minutes
Servings: 4

Ingredients

For the Chicken:
- 3-4 boneless, skinless chicken thighs
- 1 teaspoon garlic powder
- 2 teaspoons paprika
- ½ teaspoon Italian spice blend
- 1 tablespoon olive oil for cooking
- 2 teaspoons ground cumin
- ½ teaspoon red pepper flakes
- 1 teaspoon sea salt

For Rice:
- 16 ounces cauliflower rice
- Juice from ½ lemon, freshly squeezed
- 1 ½ cup chicken stock

For Garnish:
- Marinated tomatoes
- Fresh cilantro

Directions

1. Combine the entire spices for chicken in a small bowl; mix well and then rub half of it over the chicken pieces.
2. Now, over medium heat in a large skillet; heat a few tablespoons of olive oil until hot & cook the chicken pieces for 2 to 3 minutes per side, until each side turns golden brown. Remove & set aside.
3. Fill the skillet with cauliflower rice, lemon juice, stock & the leftover spice mix. Stir the cauliflower rice and then set chicken thighs on top of the rice; cover with a lid & cook until chicken is cooked through, for 15 to 20 minutes on medium-low heat.
4. Garnish with freshly chopped cilantro & lemon wedges. Serve immediately & enjoy.

Shrimp & Cauliflower Grits

Prep Time: 15 minutes
Cooking Time: 15 minutes
Servings: 4 persons

Ingredients

For Shrimp & Marinade:
- 1 ½ pounds uncooked jumbo shrimp
- ⅓ teaspoon pepper
- Juice of 1 lime, freshly squeezed
- 3 garlic cloves, crushed
- ½ cup coconut aminos
- Juice of 1 lemon, freshly squeezed
- ½ tablespoon apple cider vinegar
- 1 teaspoon ghee
- ⅓ cup light olive oil
- 1 tablespoon olive oil
- ¼ teaspoon oregano

For Garlic Cauliflower Mash:
- 1 bag of cauliflower rice or pearls
- ½ cup coconut milk, unsweetened
- 1 teaspoon pepper
- 2 tablespoon chicken stock
- 1 teaspoon kosher salt
- 1 tablespoon ghee
- ½ teaspoon chives, dry or fresh
- 1 garlic clove

For Sautéed Spinach:
- 6 cups fresh spinach
- 1 teaspoon ghee
- 2 garlic cloves
- ½ teaspoon lemon juice, fresh
- 1 tablespoon olive oil
- ½ teaspoon of each pepper & kosher salt

Directions

For Shrimp:
1. Combine the entire marinade ingredients together in a medium-sized bowl & let the shrimp to marinate for a couple of hours.
2. Now, over moderate heat in a large skillet; heat olive oil & ghee until hot. Once done; add in the shrimp & cook for 3 to 5 minutes.

For Cauliflower Mash:
1. Fill a large pot with a few inches of water & place it over high heat. Once the water starts boiling, add in the cauliflower rice.
2. Cook until tender, for 8 to 10 minutes; drain well.
3. Add the cauliflower with ghee, spices, garlic, chicken broth and coconut milk to a food processor or Vitamix.
4. Blend together until the entire ingredients are well combined. Season with pepper and salt to taste.

For Spinach:
1. Over moderate heat in a large skillet & heat the olive oil & ghee until hot.
2. Once done; add in the garlic and then throw in the spinach.
3. Squeeze lemon juice on top & sprinkle with pepper and salt. Cook for a couple of minutes, until wilted and tender.

For Shrimp & Grits:
1. Add the cauliflower mash to the bottom of a plate and then add the spinach; top with the shrimp. Squeeze fresh lemon juice on top of your recipe; serve immediately & enjoy.

Cauliflower Chickpea Masala Burgers

Prep Time: 10 minutes
Cooking Time: 25 minutes
Servings: 4

Ingredients

For the Burgers:
- 1 tablespoon ground flax seeds
- 2 garlic cloves, minced
- 1 small onion, diced
- 1 ½ cups cauliflower, finely chopped
- 2 tablespoon tomato paste
- ¼ cup fresh cilantro
- 1 can chickpeas; rinsed & drained
- ½ tablespoon turmeric
- 1 ½ tablespoon garam masala
- ½ cup panko
- Juice of ½ lemon, freshly squeezed
- 2 tablespoon vegetable oil, divided
- ½ teaspoon salt

For Cilantro-Mint Mayo:
- 1 teaspoon lemon juice, freshly squeezed
- 2 tablespoon vegan mayo
- 1 tablespoon each of fresh mint & cilantro, finely chopped

Directions

1. Whisk flax seeds with 3 tablespoons of water. Set aside & let sit for 10 to 15 minutes.
2. Over medium heat in a large skillet; heat 1 tablespoon of oil. Add and sauté the onion for 3 to 5 minutes.
3. Add cauliflower and garlic; sauté until the cauliflower softens, for 5 more minutes.
4. Transfer the cauliflower mixture to a food processor & add in the leftover burger ingredients. Pulse on high until mixed well. Make four even-sized patties from the mixture.
5. Coat the skillet with cooking spray or oil & cook the formed patties until browned, for 5 minutes per side.
6. Stir mayo ingredients together & use to top the burgers.

Cheesy Cauliflower Rice with Broccoli and Chicken

Prep Time: 15 minutes
Cooking Time: 20 minutes
Servings: 8 persons

Ingredients

- 6 cups cauliflower rice, uncooked
- 1 small red onion, chopped
- 5 tablespoon butter, divided
- 1 cup sour cream
- 3 tablespoon flour
- 1 package broccoli florets, frozen, slightly thawed (10 oz)
- 8 ounces cremini mushrooms, sliced
- 1 pound chicken breast, cut into chunks
- 3 cups whole milk
- 1 sharp cheddar cheese, shredded (8 oz)
- ¼ cup parsley, fresh, finely chopped
- 1 tablespoon fresh thyme, minced
- 3 garlic cloves, minced
- ½ teaspoon pepper
- 1 ½ teaspoon salt

Directions

1. Preheat your oven to 350 F in advance.
2. Add riced cauliflower to a large-sized mixing bowl; set aside until ready to use. Now, over medium heat in a large skillet; heat 2 tablespoon of butter until completely melted.
3. Add and sauté the onion for a couple of minutes. Add in the mushrooms & continue sautéing until mushrooms begin to turn golden brown & onions turn translucent. Add the onion mixture to the mixing bowl with the riced cauliflower.
4. Add chicken in the same skillet & continue to sauté for a couple of minutes, until browned & no longer pink. Add the sautéed chicken to the mixing bowl as well.
5. Add broccoli with cheddar cheese, sour cream & parsley to the mixing bowl. Give everything a good stir until the mixture is combined well.
6. Over medium-low heat in a large saucepan; melt the leftover butter. Add and cook the garlic for a minute. Whisk in the flour & cook for a minute more. Slowly whisk in the milk.
7. Increase the heat & bring everything together to a bubble. Stir in the thyme, pepper and salt. Continue to cook until the sauce has thickened, stirring frequently. Set aside and let slightly cool.
8. Pour the sauce on top of the cauliflower mixture and stir until everything is well combined and coated. Pour the mixture into a lightly coated 9x13" baking dish. Bake until the casserole is browned & bubbly, for 40 to 45 minutes.

Coconut Curry Chicken Meatballs with Cauliflower Rice

Prep Time: 20 minutes
Cooking Time: 30 minutes
Servings: 6

Ingredients

For the Meat Balls:
- 1 pound ground chicken
- ½ tablespoon garlic powder
- 1 teaspoon cumin
- ¼ cup rolled oats
- 1 teaspoon chili powder
- ¼ cup all-purpose flour
- 1 tablespoon dried basil
- ½ tablespoon chili paste
- 1 organic egg, large
- 1-2 tablespoons olive oil
- ⅛ teaspoon salt

For Cabbage Salad:
- 2 tablespoons rice vinegar
- ¼ cup fresh cilantro, chopped
- 4 cups purple cabbage, sliced
- Freshly squeeze lime juice
- ½ tablespoon honey
- A pinch of salt

For Curry Sauce:
- 1 can coconut milk, full-fat
- ½ tablespoon sriracha
- 1 yellow onion, sliced
- 3 tablespoons red curry paste
- 1 tablespoon garlic, minced
- 3 tablespoons lime juice, freshly squeezed
- 1 tablespoon olive oil

For Cauliflower Rice:
- 3 ½ cups riced cauliflower
- 1 tablespoon lime juice, freshly squeezed
- 2 tablespoons olive oil
- Pepper & salt to taste

Directions

1. Lightly coat a cake pan or casserole dish with the coconut oil cooking spray; set aside and then preheat your oven to 400 F in advance.
2. Prepare your cabbage salad by placing the entire ingredients together in a large bowl; mix well & then place the bowl in a fridge.
3. Prepare the meatball mixture by placing the entire ingredients into a large bowl; continue to mix until well combined.
4. Using a tablespoon cookie scoop, scoop the mixture out & mold into a small, bite-sized ball using your hands (slightly moist with water). Arrange them in oiled casserole dish.
5. Bake in the preheated oven for 8 to 10 minutes.
6. In the meantime, prepare your curry sauce by placing olive oil into a medium-sized fry pan. When hot, add & sauté the onion for a couple of minutes, then add in the remaining curry sauce ingredients. Bring everything together to a boil.
7. After 10 minutes, add curry sauce to the casserole dish with the meatballs & bake for 7 to 10 more minutes.
8. Now, add the entire ingredients for cauliflower rice into a large-sized frying pan & cook for 5 to 7 minutes.
9. When the meatballs are done, remove them from the oven & place ½ cup of the cauliflower rice, ½ cup of the cabbage salad, meatballs & curry sauce in a large bowl.
10. Top with fresh Thai basil & a squeeze of lime. Serve immediately & enjoy.

Chicken Enchilada Rice Bowls

Prep Time: 20 minutes
Cooking Time: 40 minutes
Servings: 4

Ingredients

For Red Chile Enchilada Chicken:
- 8 ounce package or can red enchilada sauce
- 4 chicken breasts, boneless, skinless
- 2 teaspoons chili powder

For Cilantro Lime Cauliflower Rice:
- 1 medium head of cauliflower, chopped into small florets
- Juice of a lime, freshly squeezed
- ¼ teaspoon garlic powder
- 2 tablespoons fresh cilantro, chopped
- 1 teaspoon chili powder
- 1 ½ teaspoons kosher salt

For Toppings:
- Black olives, black beans, tomatoes, grilled corn & fresh cilantro

Directions

For Red Chile Enchilada Chicken:
1. Add the chicken with red enchilada sauce & chili powder to a 6 quarts slow cooker.
2. Cover with a lid & set it over low-heat; cook for 4 to 6 hours, until the chicken is tender & cooked through.
3. Once the chicken is cooked through; shred using two large forks & toss in the sauce.

For Cilantro Lime Cauliflower Rice:
1. Rinse the cauliflower & pat dry.
2. Cut the cauliflower in half using a large knife & then remove the core.
3. Cut the cauliflower into large florets and then place them in the bowl of a food processor.
4. Pulse on high until you get rice or couscous like consistency.
5. Now, over moderate heat in a large skillet (coated generously with the cooking spray).
6. Add the cauliflower & then add in the garlic powder, chili powder & salt.
7. Sauté the cauliflower rice in the pan for 2 to 4 minutes, stirring frequently.
8. Squeeze in the lime juice & stir in the chopped cilantro cooking for a minute more.

For Assembling:
1. Scoop some of the cauliflower rice into the bottom of a bowl.
2. Top the rice with the black beans, grilled corn, olives, shredded chicken, tomatoes, cilantro & any toppings you desire.

Mediterranean Cauliflower Rice

Prep Time: 20 minutes
Cooking Time: 20 minutes
Servings: 4

Ingredients

- 1 medium to large sized head of cauliflower; cut into medium-sized chunks & discard the core or 16 ounces cauliflower rice, store-bought
- 2 garlic cloves, minced or pressed
- 1 tablespoon lemon juice, freshly squeezed
- ½ cup fresh flat-leaf parsley, chopped
- Freshly ground black pepper, to taste
- ½ cup almonds, sliced
- 2 tablespoons extra-virgin olive oil
- A pinch of red pepper flakes
- ¼ teaspoon fine sea salt

Directions

1. Work in batches and pulse the cauliflower chunks in a food processor until you get couscous or rice like consistency.
2. Wrap the cauliflower rice in paper towels or clean tea towels; twist & squeeze the water out as much as possible.
3. Now, over medium heat in a large skillet; toast the almonds for a couple of minutes, until fragrant & starting to turn golden on the edges, stirring frequently. Transfer the toasted almonds to a large bowl and let cool.
4. Place the skillet back to the heat & add olive oil and garlic. Cook for a couple of seconds, until the garlic is fragrant, stirring frequently. Add cauliflower rice followed by red pepper flakes & salt; give everything a good stir until combined well. Cook for a couple of minutes, until the cauliflower rice is hot & turning golden in places, stirring just after every minute or so.
5. Remove the skillet from heat and then stir in the toasted almonds, lemon juice and parsley. Season with pepper and salt to taste; serve warm & enjoy.

Thai Chicken Cauliflower Rice

Prep Time: 20 minutes
Cooking Time: 20 minutes
Servings: 4

Ingredients

- 16 ounces cauliflower rice
- 2 chicken breasts, large
- 8 ounces broccoli rabe

For Sauce:

- ⅓ cup dates, pitted
- 2 tablespoons chili paste
- ½ cup coconut aminos
- 2 garlic cloves
- ½ cup chicken stock
- Juice from 1 lime, freshly squeezed
- ½ teaspoon each of paprika & sea salt

Directions

1. Puree the entire sauce ingredients together in a high-power blender for a minute or two, until completely smooth.
2. Marinate the chicken breast in approximately ⅓ of the sauce & put in a fridge for half an hour.
3. Cook the chicken on either a skillet or grill pan. Place the chicken on a well-greased pan; cover with a lid & cook until cooked through, for 5 to 6 minutes per side.
4. Once the chicken is cooked through; remove & add broccoli to the cast iron skillet. Cook in leftover juices for a couple of minutes, until soft but ensure it's not mushy. Pour the leftover sauce in the cast iron skillet on top of the cauliflower rice & cook until soft, for 8 to 10 minutes. Serve with broccoli and chicken. Enjoy.

Beef Burrito Bowls with Cilantro Lime Rice

Prep Time: 20 minutes
Cooking Time: 20 minutes
Servings: 4

Ingredients

For the Beef:
- 1 ½ teaspoons cumin
- 1 pound lean ground beef
- 2 ½ teaspoons chili powder
- ½ teaspoon smoked paprika
- 1 ½ teaspoons onion powder
- 1 teaspoon garlic powder
- ¼ teaspoon each of pepper & salt

For the Cauliflower Rice:
- 1 pound cauliflower rice (approximately 4 cups)
- Juice of 1 lime, freshly squeezed
- ¼ cup fresh cilantro, chopped
- 2 teaspoons coconut oil
- Pepper & salt to taste

For the Guacamole:
- 2 avocados, pitted
- ¼ cup red onion, diced
- Juice of half a lime, freshly squeezed
- 2 tablespoons fresh cilantro, chopped
- 1 garlic clove, minced
- A pinch of salt

For the Pico-de-gallo:
- 2 tablespoons fresh cilantro, chopped
- 1 cup cherry tomatoes, halved
- Juice of ½ a lime, freshly squeezed
- ¼ cup red onion, diced
- A pinch of salt

For Serving:
- Plain Greek yogurt
- 4 ounces cheddar cheese, freshly grated
- Shredded romaine
- Hot sauce
- Additional chopped cilantro

Directions

1. Prepare the guacamole and pico de gallo in advance. Add tomatoes to a large bowl & add red onion, lime, cilantro & salt. Give everything a good stir until combined well & set aside.
2. Prepare the guacamole. Add avocados to a large bowl & mash with a fork. Add in the red onion, garlic, lime juice, cilantro & salt; mash until you get your desired consistency. Season with more of lime and salt to taste; set aside.
3. Preheat a medium skillet over medium to high heat. Add in the beef & cook for a few minutes. As you cook; don't forget to break it up using a large spatula. Once it begins to brown, add in the onion powder, cumin, chili powder, smoked paprika, garlic powder, pepper & salt. Give everything a good stir until combined well & cook for 5 minutes, until fully browned; set aside.
4. Now, heat a separate large-sized skillet over medium-high heat & add in the coconut oil. Add cauliflower rice & cook until heated through & tender, for 2 to 3 minutes. Add in the cilantro & lime juice; season with pepper and salt to taste.
5. To assemble: Add the cauliflower rice to a bowl and top with beef, then romaine, pico de gallo, shredded cheese, guacamole, Greek yogurt, hot sauce & more of cilantro. Serve immediately & enjoy.

Jambalaya

Prep Time: 30 minutes
Cooking Time: 45 minutes
Servings: 6

Ingredients

- 4 links Andouille sausage, halved lengthwise & sliced
- 1 bag cauliflower "rice" or "pearls" (16-ounce)
- 2 boneless, skinless chicken breast halves
- 1 large onion, finely chopped
- 2 tablespoons Cajun seasoning, divided
- 1 red bell pepper, chopped
- 4 garlic cloves, minced
- 1 can petite diced tomatoes, undrained (15-ounce)
- 2 celery stalks, chopped
- 1 tablespoon Hungarian paprika
- 8 ounces shrimp, large, peeled & deveined
- Tabasco sauce, to taste
- ¼ cup fresh parsley, chopped, divided
- 4 tablespoons olive oil, divided
- Freshly ground black pepper & salt to taste

Directions

1. Preheat your oven to 375 F in advance. Place the chicken breasts on a large-sized baking sheet, nonstick. Drizzle with approximately 1 tablespoon of olive oil. Evenly season with 2 teaspoons of Cajun seasoning, pepper & salt. Bake in the preheated oven until cooked through, for 22 to 25 minutes.
2. Place the cauliflower on a nonstick baking sheet & drizzle with 1 tablespoon of olive oil; season with 1 teaspoon Cajun seasoning, black pepper & salt. Toss well until the seasonings are distributed evenly. Roast for 8 to 10 minutes alongside the chicken.
3. In the meantime, over medium-high heat in a large sauté pan or skillet; heat the leftover oil. Add in the onion; decrease the heat & cook for 4 to 5 minutes. Add in the red bell pepper and celery; continue to cook until very soft, for 7 to 8 minutes. Keep heat at medium heat.
4. Add the Andouille sausage, paprika & garlic; cook for a minute or two. Add in the shrimp and tomatoes; cook until the shrimp is cooked through, stirring often.
5. Cut the chicken into ½" pieces. Add to the pan along with cauliflower & cook until heated through. Add Tabasco sauce; stir well. Taste and adjust the amount of seasonings to preference.
6. Add half of the parsley. Transfer to a large-sized serving platter & garnish with the leftover parsley.

Gumbo and Rice

Prep Time: 15 minutes
Cooking Time: 35 minutes
Servings: 4

Ingredients

- A head of large cauliflower
- 1 pound chicken (rotisserie), diced
- 2 Andouille sausage segmented
- 1 pound cooked Shrimp
- 8 garlic cloves, minced
- 1 can crushed tomatoes (14 oz.)
- 2 green bell peppers, diced
- 1 zucchini, large, diced
- 2 tablespoon Cajun seasoning
- 1 okra, diced
- 4 tablespoon olive oil
- 1 cup chicken broth

Directions

1. Prepare the Cauliflower Rice: Cut the head of cauliflower into four equal-sized sections. Grate the cauliflower into rice using a grater & press out the moisture using paper towels. Now, over moderate heat in a large frying pan; heat the oil until hot and then, pour in the cauliflower; stir well & cook for 3 to 5 minutes, covered.
2. For Shrimp: Over medium high heat in a large frying pan; heat 1 tablespoon of olive oil until hot. Once done; add 2 minced garlic cloves to the hot pan & cook for 8 to 10 seconds. Add shrimp; stir well & cook for 2 minutes per side; remove and set aside.
3. Place the pot over moderate heat on stove. Once hot, add 2 tablespoons of olive oil and then add onions & andouille sausage. Cook until onions just begin to turn brown, for 8 to 10 minutes, stirring occasionally.
4. Add 6 minced garlic cloves & stir for a minute.
5. Mix in the green bell peppers, crushed tomatoes, zucchini, okra, chicken broth and Cajun seasoning.
6. Increased the heat to high & bring everything together to a boil. Once it starts boiling, decrease the heat to low & let simmer for 12 to 15 minutes, uncovered.
7. Add in the shrimp and chicken, stir together & let simmer for 5 more minutes.
8. Add in the cauliflower rice & gumbo to the bowl; serve immediately & enjoy.

Desserts

Cauliflower Rice Pudding

Prep Time: 10 minutes
Cooking Time: 10 minutes
Servings: 2

Ingredients

- 3½ cups riced cauliflower
- ¼ cup egg whites, boxed
- 3 teaspoon cinnamon
- 1 cup coconut or almond, rice milk (boxed)
- 2 packets of liquid stevia or to taste

Directions

1. Over medium heat in a large sauce pan; combine 1½ cup of riced cauliflower with the milk
2. Add in the leftover ingredients & bring everything together to a simmer; let simmer for 4 to 5 minutes.
3. Add in the leftover riced cauliflower and stir until you get your desired consistency.
4. Decrease the heat to low and cook for a couple of more minutes, until thickened, stirring constantly.
5. Cover & cook until thicken
6. Serve hot & enjoy.

Cauliflower Chocolate Pudding

Prep Time: 5 minutes
Cooking Time: 20 minutes
Servings: 2

Ingredients

- 2 cups riced cauliflower
- 1 teaspoon vanilla extract
- 3 tablespoon unsweetened cocoa
- ¼ cup egg whites
- 1 cup almond milk
- ⅓ cup sugar

Directions

1. Over moderate heat in a large sauce pan; combine 1 ½ cup of Riced Cauliflower with almond milk, add in the leftover ingredients & bring everything together to a simmer for 4 to 5 minutes.
2. Add in the leftover Riced Cauliflower and continue to stir until you get your desired consistency.
3. Decrease the heat to low; continue to stir for a couple of more minutes, until thickened.
4. Cover & refrigerate for overnight.

Chocolate Cauliflower Bars

Prep Time: 10 minutes
Cooking Time: 10 minutes
Servings: 16

Ingredients

- 2 cups cauliflower florets
- ⅓ cup coconut sugar
- 1 cup ground walnuts
- ¼ cup raw cacao powder
- 1 tablespoon ground flaxseed
- ½ cup buckwheat flour
- 1 teaspoon cinnamon
- 2 tablespoon coconut oil
- A pinch of sea salt

Optional toppings:
- Raw cacao nibs
- 50g dark chocolate

Directions

1. Steam or boil the cauliflower until soft; drain well & blend until completely smooth then, stir in the coconut oil; set aside.
2. Line a standard-sized 9x 9" square baking dish with the baking paper and preheat your oven to 360 F in advance. Whisk the buckwheat flour with coconut sugar, ground walnuts, flaxseed, cacao powder, cinnamon & sea salt in a large bowl.
3. Add dry ingredients to the cauliflower; give everything a good stir until well combined. Spoon the mixture into the prepared baking dish & level the surface. Bake in the preheated oven until firm in the center, for 30 minutes.
4. Set aside and let cool down completely then cut into 16 bars. Melt the dark chocolate in double boiler & drizzle on top of the bars. Sprinkle with some raw cacao nibs. Store in an airtight container in a fridge. Enjoy.

Chewy Chocolate Chip Cookies with Cauliflower

Prep Time: 15 minutes
Cooking Time: 20 minutes
Servings: 24

Ingredients

- 1 cup Cauliflower "Rice" (micro-waved for 5 minutes, uncovered)
- ½ cup walnuts, chopped
- 1 ½ cup all-purpose flour
- ¾ cup sugar
- 1 teaspoon vanilla extract
- ½ cup softened butter, unsalted
- 1 teaspoon baking soda
- ¾ cup mini chocolate chips, semi-sweet
- 1 organic egg, large
- ½ teaspoon salt

Directions

1. Preheat your oven to 350 F in advance. Microwave the riced cauliflower; set aside at room temperature to cool.
2. Cream butter with sugar in a large-sized mixing bowl for a minute or two, until light & fluffy. Add vanilla and egg; beat until well incorporated and then stir in the cooked "Rice".
3. Whisk the flour with baking soda and salt in a separate small bowl. Add dry ingredients to the butter mixture; mix until just blended and then add in the nuts and chocolate chips; continue to mix until blended well.
4. For small cookies; drop a tablespoon of the mixture (2" apart) & for larger cookies; drop 2 tablespoons of the mixture (approximately 3" apart) onto the cookie sheets lined with parchment; pressing the cookies flat. Bake in the preheated oven until golden brown, for 9 to 12 minutes. Serve and enjoy.

Get Free Recipe eBooks!
Cookbook Club

Fabulous Free eBook Cookbooks Every Week!

Our eBooks are FREE for the first few days publication. Be the first to know when new books are published. Our collection includes hundreds of books on topics including healthy foods, diets, food allergy alternatives, gourmet meals, desserts, and easy and inexpensive meals.

Join the mailing list at:
EncoreBookClub.com

Related Books
Appetizers
http://url80.com/appetizers
Boozy Desserts
http://url80.com/boozy
Crazy for Cupcakes
http://url80.com/cupcakes
Fair Foods
http://url80.com/fair
Guacamole
http://url80.com/guacamole
Scones
http://url80.com/scones
Smoothies
http://url80.com/smoothies
Sriracha
http://url80.com/sriracha
Ramen Recipes
http://url80.com/ramen
Porkalicious
http://url80.com/porkalicious
Pudding
http://url80.com/pudding
The Awesome Avocado
http://url80.com/avocado

Thank You for Your Purchase!

We know you have many choices when it comes to ready and recipe books. Your patronage is sincerely appreciated. If you would like to provide us feedback, go to http://url80.com/feedback.

Please Consider Writing an Amazon Review!

Happy with this book? If so, please consider writing a positive review. It helps others know it's a quality book and allows us to continue to promote our positive message. To write reviews, go to http://url80.com/reviews.

Thank You!

Made in the USA
Monee, IL
20 September 2019